365 Days

A Planner for

Every Day of the Year

Activinotes

Activinotes

DAILY JOURNALS, PLANNERS, NOTEBOOKS AND OTHER BLANK BOOKS

things to do:

_____ ☐
_____ ☐
_____ ☐
_____ ☐
_____ ☐
_____ ☐
_____ ☐
_____ ☐

date
____

_____ ☐
_____ ☐
_____ ☐
_____ ☐
_____ ☐

notes:

_____
_____
_____
_____
_____

time	task	comments	status

things to do:

_____ ☐
_____ ☐
_____ ☐
_____ ☐
_____ ☐
_____ ☐
_____ ☐
_____ ☐

date
____

_____ ☐
_____ ☐
_____ ☐
_____ ☐
_____ ☐

notes:

_____
_____
_____
_____
_____

time	task	comments	status

things to do:

_____ ☐
_____ ☐
_____ ☐
_____ ☐
_____ ☐
_____ ☐
_____ ☐
_____ ☐

date
_____

_____ ☐
_____ ☐
_____ ☐
_____ ☐
_____ ☐

notes:

_____
_____
_____
_____
_____

time	task	comments	status

things to do:

_____ ☐
_____ ☐
_____ ☐
_____ ☐
_____ ☐
_____ ☐
_____ ☐
_____ ☐

_____ ☐
_____ ☐
_____ ☐
_____ ☐
_____ ☐

date
_____

notes:

_____
_____
_____
_____
_____

time	task	comments	status

things to do:

_____ ☐
_____ ☐
_____ ☐
_____ ☐
_____ ☐
_____ ☐
_____ ☐
_____ ☐

date
____

_____ ☐
_____ ☐
_____ ☐
_____ ☐
_____ ☐

notes:
_____
_____
_____
_____
_____

time	task	comments	status

things to do:

_____ ☐
_____ ☐
_____ ☐
_____ ☐
_____ ☐
_____ ☐
_____ ☐
_____ ☐

date
_____

_____ ☐
_____ ☐
_____ ☐
_____ ☐
_____ ☐

notes:

_____
_____
_____
_____
_____

time	task	comments	status

things to do:

_____ ☐
_____ ☐
_____ ☐
_____ ☐
_____ ☐
_____ ☐
_____ ☐
_____ ☐

date
_____

_____ ☐
_____ ☐
_____ ☐
_____ ☐
_____ ☐

notes:

_____
_____
_____
_____
_____

time	task	comments	status

things to do:

_____ ☐
_____ ☐
_____ ☐
_____ ☐
_____ ☐
_____ ☐
_____ ☐
_____ ☐

date
____

_____ ☐
_____ ☐
_____ ☐
_____ ☐
_____ ☐

notes:

_____
_____
_____
_____
_____

time	task	comments	status

things to do:

_____ ☐
_____ ☐
_____ ☐
_____ ☐
_____ ☐
_____ ☐
_____ ☐
_____ ☐

date
____

_____ ☐
_____ ☐
_____ ☐
_____ ☐
_____ ☐

notes:

_____
_____
_____
_____
_____

time	task	comments	status

things to do:

date
_____

notes:
_____
_____
_____
_____
_____

time	task	comments	status

things to do:

_____ ☐
_____ ☐
_____ ☐
_____ ☐
_____ ☐
_____ ☐
_____ ☐
_____ ☐

date
____

_____ ☐
_____ ☐
_____ ☐
_____ ☐
_____ ☐

notes:

_____
_____
_____
_____
_____

time	task	comments	status

things to do:

_____ ☐
_____ ☐
_____ ☐
_____ ☐
_____ ☐
_____ ☐
_____ ☐
_____ ☐

date
_____

_____ ☐
_____ ☐
_____ ☐
_____ ☐
_____ ☐

notes:

_____
_____
_____
_____
_____

time	task	comments	status

things to do:

_____ ☐
_____ ☐
_____ ☐
_____ ☐
_____ ☐
_____ ☐
_____ ☐
_____ ☐

date
____

_____ ☐
_____ ☐
_____ ☐
_____ ☐
_____ ☐

notes:

_____
_____
_____
_____
_____

time	task	comments	status

things to do:

_____ ☐
_____ ☐
_____ ☐
_____ ☐
_____ ☐
_____ ☐
_____ ☐
_____ ☐

date
_____

_____ ☐
_____ ☐
_____ ☐
_____ ☐
_____ ☐

notes:

_____
_____
_____
_____
_____

time	task	comments	status

things to do:

_____ ☐
_____ ☐
_____ ☐
_____ ☐
_____ ☐
_____ ☐
_____ ☐
_____ ☐

date
_____

_____ ☐
_____ ☐
_____ ☐
_____ ☐
_____ ☐

notes:

_____
_____
_____
_____
_____

time	task	comments	status

things to do:

_____ ☐
_____ ☐
_____ ☐
_____ ☐
_____ ☐
_____ ☐
_____ ☐
_____ ☐

date
_____

_____ ☐
_____ ☐
_____ ☐
_____ ☐
_____ ☐

notes:

_____

_____

_____

_____

_____

time	task	comments	status

things to do:

_____ ☐
_____ ☐
_____ ☐
_____ ☐
_____ ☐
_____ ☐
_____ ☐
_____ ☐

date
____

_____ ☐
_____ ☐
_____ ☐
_____ ☐
_____ ☐

notes:

_____
_____
_____
_____
_____

time	task	comments	status

things to do:

_____ ☐
_____ ☐
_____ ☐
_____ ☐
_____ ☐
_____ ☐
_____ ☐
_____ ☐

date
_____

_____ ☐
_____ ☐
_____ ☐
_____ ☐
_____ ☐

notes:

_____
_____
_____
_____
_____

time	task	comments	status

things to do:

_____ ☐
_____ ☐
_____ ☐
_____ ☐   _____ ☐
_____ ☐   _____ ☐
_____ ☐   _____ ☐
_____ ☐   _____ ☐
_____ ☐   _____ ☐

date
_____

notes:

_____
_____
_____
_____
_____

time	task	comments	status

things to do:

_____ ☐
_____ ☐
_____ ☐
_____ ☐
_____ ☐
_____ ☐
_____ ☐
_____ ☐

date
_____

_____ ☐
_____ ☐
_____ ☐
_____ ☐
_____ ☐
_____ ☐

notes:

_____
_____
_____
_____
_____

time	task	comments	status

things to do:

_____ ☐
_____ ☐
_____ ☐
_____ ☐
_____ ☐   _____ ☐
_____ ☐   _____ ☐
_____ ☐   _____ ☐
_____ ☐   _____ ☐
_____ ☐   _____ ☐

date
_____

notes:

_____
_____
_____
_____
_____

time	task	comments	status

things to do:

_____ ☐
_____ ☐
_____ ☐
_____ ☐
_____ ☐
_____ ☐
_____ ☐
_____ ☐

date
_____

_____ ☐
_____ ☐
_____ ☐
_____ ☐
_____ ☐

notes:

_____
_____
_____
_____
_____

time	task	comments	status

things to do:

_____ ☐
_____ ☐
_____ ☐
_____ ☐
_____ ☐
_____ ☐
_____ ☐
_____ ☐

date
_____

_____ ☐
_____ ☐
_____ ☐
_____ ☐
_____ ☐

notes:

_____
_____
_____
_____
_____

time	task	comments	status

things to do:

_____ ☐
_____ ☐
_____ ☐
_____ ☐
_____ ☐
_____ ☐
_____ ☐
_____ ☐

date
_____

_____ ☐
_____ ☐
_____ ☐
_____ ☐
_____ ☐

notes:
_____
_____
_____
_____
_____

time	task	comments	status

things to do:

_____ ☐
_____ ☐
_____ ☐
_____ ☐
_____ ☐
_____ ☐
_____ ☐
_____ ☐

date
_____

_____ ☐
_____ ☐
_____ ☐
_____ ☐
_____ ☐

notes:

_____
_____
_____
_____
_____

time	task	comments	status

things to do:

_____ ☐
_____ ☐
_____ ☐
_____ ☐
_____ ☐
_____ ☐
_____ ☐
_____ ☐

date
____

_____ ☐
_____ ☐
_____ ☐
_____ ☐
_____ ☐

notes:

_____
_____
_____
_____
_____

time	task	comments	status

things to do:

_____ ☐
_____ ☐
_____ ☐
_____ ☐
_____ ☐
_____ ☐
_____ ☐
_____ ☐

date
_____

_____ ☐
_____ ☐
_____ ☐
_____ ☐
_____ ☐

notes:

_____
_____
_____
_____
_____

time	task	comments	status

things to do:

_____ ☐
_____ ☐
_____ ☐
_____ ☐
_____ ☐
_____ ☐
_____ ☐
_____ ☐

date
_____

_____ ☐
_____ ☐
_____ ☐
_____ ☐
_____ ☐

notes:

_____
_____
_____
_____
_____

time	task	comments	status

things to do:

_____ ☐
_____ ☐
_____ ☐
_____ ☐
_____ ☐
_____ ☐
_____ ☐
_____ ☐

date
____

_____ ☐
_____ ☐
_____ ☐
_____ ☐
_____ ☐

notes:

_____
_____
_____
_____
_____

time	task	comments	status

things to do:

_____ ☐
_____ ☐
_____ ☐
_____ ☐
_____ ☐
_____ ☐
_____ ☐
_____ ☐

date
_____

_____ ☐
_____ ☐
_____ ☐
_____ ☐
_____ ☐

notes:

_____
_____
_____
_____
_____

time	task	comments	status

things to do:

_____ ☐
_____ ☐
_____ ☐
_____ ☐
_____ ☐
_____ ☐
_____ ☐
_____ ☐

date
___

_____ ☐
_____ ☐
_____ ☐
_____ ☐
_____ ☐

notes:

_____
_____
_____
_____
_____

time	task	comments	status

things to do:

_____ ☐
_____ ☐
_____ ☐
_____ ☐
_____ ☐
_____ ☐
_____ ☐
_____ ☐

date
____

_____ ☐
_____ ☐
_____ ☐
_____ ☐
_____ ☐

notes:

_____
_____
_____
_____
_____

time	task	comments	status

things to do:

_____ ☐
_____ ☐
_____ ☐
_____ ☐
_____ ☐
_____ ☐
_____ ☐
_____ ☐

date
_____

_____ ☐
_____ ☐
_____ ☐
_____ ☐
_____ ☐

notes:

_____
_____
_____
_____
_____

time	task	comments	status

things to do:

_____ ☐
_____ ☐
_____ ☐
_____ ☐
_____ ☐
_____ ☐
_____ ☐
_____ ☐

date
____

_____ ☐
_____ ☐
_____ ☐
_____ ☐
_____ ☐

notes:

_____
_____
_____
_____
_____

time	task	comments	status

things to do:

_____ ☐
_____ ☐
_____ ☐
_____ ☐
_____ ☐
_____ ☐
_____ ☐
_____ ☐

date
_____

_____ ☐
_____ ☐
_____ ☐
_____ ☐
_____ ☐

notes:

_____
_____
_____
_____
_____

time	task	comments	status

things to do:

_____ ☐
_____ ☐
_____ ☐
_____ ☐
_____ ☐
_____ ☐
_____ ☐
_____ ☐

date
____

_____ ☐
_____ ☐
_____ ☐
_____ ☐
_____ ☐

notes:

_____
_____
_____
_____
_____

time	task	comments	status

things to do:

_____ ☐
_____ ☐
_____ ☐
_____ ☐
_____ ☐
_____ ☐
_____ ☐
_____ ☐

date
_____

_____ ☐
_____ ☐
_____ ☐
_____ ☐
_____ ☐

notes:

_____
_____
_____
_____
_____

time	task	comments	status

things to do:

_____ ☐
_____ ☐
_____ ☐
_____ ☐
_____ ☐
_____ ☐
_____ ☐
_____ ☐

date
____

_____ ☐
_____ ☐
_____ ☐
_____ ☐
_____ ☐

notes:

_____
_____
_____
_____
_____

time	task	comments	status

things to do:

_____ ☐
_____ ☐
_____ ☐
_____ ☐
_____ ☐
_____ ☐
_____ ☐
_____ ☐

date
_____

_____ ☐
_____ ☐
_____ ☐
_____ ☐
_____ ☐

notes:

_____
_____
_____
_____
_____

time	task	comments	status

things to do:

_____ ☐
_____ ☐
_____ ☐
_____ ☐
_____ ☐
_____ ☐
_____ ☐
_____ ☐

date
_____

_____ ☐
_____ ☐
_____ ☐
_____ ☐
_____ ☐

notes:

_____
_____
_____
_____
_____

time	task	comments	status

things to do:

_____ ☐
_____ ☐
_____ ☐
_____ ☐
_____ ☐
_____ ☐
_____ ☐
_____ ☐

date
____

_____ ☐
_____ ☐
_____ ☐
_____ ☐
_____ ☐

notes:

_____
_____
_____
_____
_____

time	task	comments	status

things to do:

_____ ☐
_____ ☐
_____ ☐
_____ ☐
_____ ☐
_____ ☐
_____ ☐
_____ ☐

date
_____

_____ ☐
_____ ☐
_____ ☐
_____ ☐
_____ ☐

notes:

_____
_____
_____
_____
_____

time	task	comments	status

things to do:

_____ ☐
_____ ☐
_____ ☐
_____ ☐
_____ ☐
_____ ☐
_____ ☐
_____ ☐

date
_____

_____ ☐
_____ ☐
_____ ☐
_____ ☐
_____ ☐

notes:

_____
_____
_____
_____
_____

time	task	comments	status

things to do:

_____ ☐
_____ ☐
_____ ☐
_____ ☐
_____ ☐
_____ ☐
_____ ☐
_____ ☐

date
____

_____ ☐
_____ ☐
_____ ☐
_____ ☐
_____ ☐

notes:

_____
_____
_____
_____
_____

time	task	comments	status

things to do:

_____ ☐
_____ ☐
_____ ☐
_____ ☐
_____ ☐
_____ ☐
_____ ☐
_____ ☐

date
____

_____ ☐
_____ ☐
_____ ☐
_____ ☐
_____ ☐

notes:
_____
_____
_____
_____

time	task	comments	status

things to do:

_____ ☐
_____ ☐
_____ ☐
_____ ☐
_____ ☐
_____ ☐
_____ ☐
_____ ☐

date
_____

_____ ☐
_____ ☐
_____ ☐
_____ ☐
_____ ☐

notes:

_____
_____
_____
_____
_____

time	task	comments	status

things to do:

_____ ☐
_____ ☐
_____ ☐
_____ ☐
_____ ☐
_____ ☐
_____ ☐
_____ ☐

date
_____

_____ ☐
_____ ☐
_____ ☐
_____ ☐
_____ ☐

notes:

_____
_____
_____
_____
_____

time	task	comments	status

things to do:

_____ ☐
_____ ☐
_____ ☐
_____ ☐
_____ ☐
_____ ☐
_____ ☐
_____ ☐

date
_____

_____ ☐
_____ ☐
_____ ☐
_____ ☐
_____ ☐

notes:

_____
_____
_____
_____
_____

time	task	comments	status

things to do:

_____ ☐
_____ ☐
_____ ☐
_____ ☐
_____ ☐
_____ ☐
_____ ☐
_____ ☐

date
_____

_____ ☐
_____ ☐
_____ ☐
_____ ☐
_____ ☐

notes:
_____
_____
_____
_____
_____

time	task	comments	status

things to do:
_____ ☐
_____ ☐
_____ ☐
_____ ☐
_____ ☐
_____ ☐
_____ ☐
_____ ☐

date
_____

_____ ☐
_____ ☐
_____ ☐
_____ ☐

notes:
_____
_____
_____
_____
_____

time	task	comments	status

things to do:

_____ ☐
_____ ☐
_____ ☐
_____ ☐
_____ ☐
_____ ☐
_____ ☐
_____ ☐

_____ ☐
_____ ☐
_____ ☐
_____ ☐
_____ ☐

date
_____

notes:

_____
_____
_____
_____
_____

time	task	comments	status

things to do:

_____ ☐
_____ ☐
_____ ☐
_____ ☐
_____ ☐
_____ ☐
_____ ☐
_____ ☐

date
_____

_____ ☐
_____ ☐
_____ ☐
_____ ☐
_____ ☐

notes:

_____
_____
_____
_____
_____
_____

time	task	comments	status

things to do:

_____ ☐
_____ ☐
_____ ☐
_____ ☐
_____ ☐
_____ ☐
_____ ☐
_____ ☐

date
___

_____ ☐
_____ ☐
_____ ☐
_____ ☐
_____ ☐

notes:

_____
_____
_____
_____
_____

time	task	comments	status

things to do:

_____ ☐
_____ ☐
_____ ☐
_____ ☐
_____ ☐
_____ ☐
_____ ☐
_____ ☐

date
____

_____ ☐
_____ ☐
_____ ☐
_____ ☐
_____ ☐

notes:

_____
_____
_____
_____
_____

time	task	comments	status

things to do:

_____ □
_____ □
_____ □
_____ □
_____ □
_____ □
_____ □
_____ □

date
_____

_____ □
_____ □
_____ □
_____ □
_____ □

notes:
_____
_____
_____
_____
_____
_____

time	task	comments	status

things to do:

_____ ☐
_____ ☐
_____ ☐
_____ ☐
_____ ☐
_____ ☐
_____ ☐
_____ ☐

date
____

_____ ☐
_____ ☐
_____ ☐
_____ ☐
_____ ☐

notes:

_____
_____
_____
_____
_____

time	task	comments	status

things to do:

_____ ☐
_____ ☐
_____ ☐
_____ ☐
_____ ☐
_____ ☐
_____ ☐
_____ ☐

date
_____

_____ ☐
_____ ☐
_____ ☐
_____ ☐
_____ ☐

notes:

_____
_____
_____
_____
_____

time	task	comments	status

things to do:

_____ ☐
_____ ☐
_____ ☐
_____ ☐
_____ ☐
_____ ☐
_____ ☐
_____ ☐

date
_____

_____ ☐
_____ ☐
_____ ☐
_____ ☐
_____ ☐

notes:

_____
_____
_____
_____
_____

time	*task*	*comments*	*status*

things to do:

_____ ☐
_____ ☐
_____ ☐
_____ ☐
_____ ☐
_____ ☐
_____ ☐
_____ ☐

date
____

_____ ☐
_____ ☐
_____ ☐
_____ ☐
_____ ☐

notes:

_____
_____
_____
_____
_____

time	task	comments	status

things to do:

_____ ☐
_____ ☐
_____ ☐
_____ ☐
_____ ☐
_____ ☐
_____ ☐
_____ ☐

date
_____

_____ ☐
_____ ☐
_____ ☐
_____ ☐
_____ ☐

notes:

_____
_____
_____
_____
_____

time	task	comments	status

things to do:

_____ ☐
_____ ☐
_____ ☐
_____ ☐
_____ ☐
_____ ☐
_____ ☐
_____ ☐

date
_____

_____ ☐
_____ ☐
_____ ☐
_____ ☐
_____ ☐

notes:
_____
_____
_____
_____
_____

time	task	comments	status

things to do:

_____ ☐
_____ ☐
_____ ☐
_____ ☐
_____ ☐
_____ ☐
_____ ☐
_____ ☐

date
_____

_____ ☐
_____ ☐
_____ ☐
_____ ☐
_____ ☐

notes:

_____
_____
_____
_____
_____

time	task	comments	status

things to do:

_____ ☐
_____ ☐
_____ ☐
_____ ☐
_____ ☐
_____ ☐
_____ ☐
_____ ☐

_____ ☐
_____ ☐
_____ ☐
_____ ☐
_____ ☐

date
_____

notes:

_____
_____
_____
_____
_____

time	task	comments	status

things to do:

_____ ☐
_____ ☐
_____ ☐
_____ ☐
_____ ☐
_____ ☐
_____ ☐
_____ ☐

date
_____

_____ ☐
_____ ☐
_____ ☐
_____ ☐
_____ ☐

notes:

_____
_____
_____
_____
_____

time	task	comments	status

things to do:

_____ ☐
_____ ☐
_____ ☐
_____ ☐
_____ ☐
_____ ☐
_____ ☐
_____ ☐

date
____

_____ ☐
_____ ☐
_____ ☐
_____ ☐
_____ ☐

notes:

_____
_____
_____
_____
_____
_____

time	task	comments	status

things to do:

_____ ☐
_____ ☐
_____ ☐
_____ ☐
_____ ☐
_____ ☐
_____ ☐
_____ ☐

date
_____

_____ ☐
_____ ☐
_____ ☐
_____ ☐
_____ ☐

notes:
_____
_____
_____
_____
_____

time	task	comments	status

things to do:

_____ ☐
_____ ☐
_____ ☐
_____ ☐
_____ ☐
_____ ☐
_____ ☐
_____ ☐

date
_____

_____ ☐
_____ ☐
_____ ☐
_____ ☐
_____ ☐

notes:

_____
_____
_____
_____
_____

time	task	comments	status

things to do:

_____ ☐
_____ ☐
_____ ☐
_____ ☐
_____ ☐
_____ ☐
_____ ☐
_____ ☐

date
_____

_____ ☐
_____ ☐
_____ ☐
_____ ☐
_____ ☐

notes:

_____
_____
_____
_____
_____

time	task	comments	status

things to do:

_____ ☐
_____ ☐
_____ ☐
_____ ☐
_____ ☐
_____ ☐
_____ ☐
_____ ☐

date
_____

_____ ☐
_____ ☐
_____ ☐
_____ ☐
_____ ☐

notes:

_____
_____
_____
_____
_____

time	task	comments	status

things to do:

_____ ☐
_____ ☐
_____ ☐
_____ ☐
_____ ☐
_____ ☐
_____ ☐
_____ ☐

date
_____

_____ ☐
_____ ☐
_____ ☐
_____ ☐
_____ ☐

notes:

_____
_____
_____
_____
_____

time	task	comments	status

things to do:

_____ ☐
_____ ☐
_____ ☐
_____ ☐
_____ ☐
_____ ☐
_____ ☐
_____ ☐

date
_____

_____ ☐
_____ ☐
_____ ☐
_____ ☐
_____ ☐

notes:

_____
_____
_____
_____
_____

time	task	comments	status

things to do:

_____ ☐
_____ ☐
_____ ☐
_____ ☐
_____ ☐
_____ ☐
_____ ☐
_____ ☐

date
____

_____ ☐
_____ ☐
_____ ☐
_____ ☐
_____ ☐

notes:

_____
_____
_____
_____
_____

time	task	comments	status

things to do:

_____ ☐
_____ ☐
_____ ☐
_____ ☐
_____ ☐
_____ ☐
_____ ☐
_____ ☐

date
_____

_____ ☐
_____ ☐
_____ ☐
_____ ☐
_____ ☐

notes:

_____
_____
_____
_____
_____

time	task	comments	status

things to do:

_____ ☐
_____ ☐
_____ ☐
_____ ☐
_____ ☐
_____ ☐
_____ ☐
_____ ☐

date
_____

_____ ☐
_____ ☐
_____ ☐
_____ ☐
_____ ☐

notes:

_____
_____
_____
_____
_____

time	task	comments	status

things to do:

_____ ☐
_____ ☐
_____ ☐
_____ ☐
_____ ☐
_____ ☐
_____ ☐
_____ ☐

date
_____

_____ ☐
_____ ☐
_____ ☐
_____ ☐
_____ ☐

notes:

_____
_____
_____
_____
_____

time	task	comments	status

things to do:

_____ ☐
_____ ☐
_____ ☐
_____ ☐
_____ ☐
_____ ☐
_____ ☐
_____ ☐

date
_____

_____ ☐
_____ ☐
_____ ☐
_____ ☐
_____ ☐

notes:

_____
_____
_____
_____
_____

time	task	comments	status

things to do:

_____ ☐
_____ ☐
_____ ☐
_____ ☐
_____ ☐
_____ ☐
_____ ☐
_____ ☐

date
____

_____ ☐
_____ ☐
_____ ☐
_____ ☐
_____ ☐

notes:

_____
_____
_____
_____
_____

time	task	comments	status

things to do:

_____ ☐
_____ ☐
_____ ☐
_____ ☐
_____ ☐
_____ ☐
_____ ☐
_____ ☐

date
_____

_____ ☐
_____ ☐
_____ ☐
_____ ☐
_____ ☐

notes:

_____
_____
_____
_____
_____

time	task	comments	status

things to do:

_____ ☐
_____ ☐
_____ ☐
_____ ☐
_____ ☐
_____ ☐
_____ ☐
_____ ☐

date
_____

_____ ☐
_____ ☐
_____ ☐
_____ ☐
_____ ☐

notes:

_____
_____
_____
_____
_____

time	task	comments	status

things to do:

_____ ☐
_____ ☐
_____ ☐
_____ ☐
_____ ☐
_____ ☐
_____ ☐
_____ ☐

date
_____

_____ ☐
_____ ☐
_____ ☐
_____ ☐
_____ ☐

notes:
_____
_____
_____
_____
_____

time	task	comments	status

things to do:

_____ ☐
_____ ☐
_____ ☐
_____ ☐
_____ ☐
_____ ☐
_____ ☐
_____ ☐

date
_____

_____ ☐
_____ ☐
_____ ☐
_____ ☐
_____ ☐

notes:

_____
_____
_____
_____
_____

time	task	comments	status

things to do:

_____ ☐
_____ ☐
_____ ☐
_____ ☐
_____ ☐
_____ ☐
_____ ☐
_____ ☐

date
_____

_____ ☐
_____ ☐
_____ ☐
_____ ☐
_____ ☐

notes:

_____
_____
_____
_____
_____

time	_task_	_comments_	_status_

things to do:

_____ ☐
_____ ☐
_____ ☐
_____ ☐
_____ ☐
_____ ☐
_____ ☐
_____ ☐

date
_____

_____ ☐
_____ ☐
_____ ☐
_____ ☐
_____ ☐

notes:

_____
_____
_____
_____
_____

time	task	comments	status

things to do:

_____ ☐
_____ ☐
_____ ☐
_____ ☐
_____ ☐
_____ ☐
_____ ☐
_____ ☐

date
_____

_____ ☐
_____ ☐
_____ ☐
_____ ☐
_____ ☐

notes:

_____
_____
_____
_____
_____
_____

time	task	comments	status

things to do:

_____ ☐
_____ ☐
_____ ☐
_____ ☐
_____ ☐
_____ ☐
_____ ☐
_____ ☐

date
_____

_____ ☐
_____ ☐
_____ ☐
_____ ☐
_____ ☐

notes:

_____
_____
_____
_____
_____

time	task	comments	status

things to do:

_____ ☐
_____ ☐
_____ ☐
_____ ☐
_____ ☐
_____ ☐
_____ ☐
_____ ☐

date
____

_____ ☐
_____ ☐
_____ ☐
_____ ☐
_____ ☐

notes:

_____
_____
_____
_____
_____

time	task	comments	status

things to do:

_____ ☐
_____ ☐
_____ ☐
_____ ☐
_____ ☐
_____ ☐
_____ ☐
_____ ☐

date
____

_____ ☐
_____ ☐
_____ ☐
_____ ☐
_____ ☐

notes:

_____
_____
_____
_____
_____
_____

time	task	comments	status

things to do:

_____ ☐
_____ ☐
_____ ☐
_____ ☐
_____ ☐
_____ ☐
_____ ☐
_____ ☐

date
_____

_____ ☐
_____ ☐
_____ ☐
_____ ☐
_____ ☐

notes:

_____
_____
_____
_____
_____

time	task	comments	status

things to do:

date
_____

_____ ☐
_____ ☐
_____ ☐
_____ ☐
_____ ☐
_____ ☐
_____ ☐
_____ ☐

_____ ☐
_____ ☐
_____ ☐
_____ ☐
_____ ☐

notes:

_____
_____
_____
_____
_____

time	task	comments	status

things to do:

_____ ☐
_____ ☐
_____ ☐
_____ ☐
_____ ☐
_____ ☐
_____ ☐
_____ ☐

date
_____

_____ ☐
_____ ☐
_____ ☐
_____ ☐
_____ ☐

notes:

_____
_____
_____
_____
_____

time	task	comments	status

things to do:

_____ ☐
_____ ☐
_____ ☐
_____ ☐
_____ ☐
_____ ☐
_____ ☐
_____ ☐

date
_____

_____ ☐
_____ ☐
_____ ☐
_____ ☐
_____ ☐

notes:

_____
_____
_____
_____
_____

time	task	comments	status

things to do:

_____ ☐
_____ ☐
_____ ☐
_____ ☐
_____ ☐
_____ ☐
_____ ☐
_____ ☐

date
_____

_____ ☐
_____ ☐
_____ ☐
_____ ☐
_____ ☐

notes:

_____
_____
_____
_____
_____

time	task	comments	status

things to do:

_____ ☐
_____ ☐
_____ ☐
_____ ☐
_____ ☐
_____ ☐
_____ ☐
_____ ☐

date
_____

_____ ☐
_____ ☐
_____ ☐
_____ ☐
_____ ☐

notes:
_____
_____
_____
_____
_____

time	task	comments	status

things to do:

_____ ☐
_____ ☐
_____ ☐
_____ ☐
_____ ☐
_____ ☐
_____ ☐
_____ ☐

date
____

_____ ☐
_____ ☐
_____ ☐
_____ ☐
_____ ☐

notes:

_____
_____
_____
_____
_____

time	task	comments	status

things to do:

_____ ☐
_____ ☐
_____ ☐
_____ ☐
_____ ☐
_____ ☐
_____ ☐
_____ ☐

date
____

_____ ☐
_____ ☐
_____ ☐
_____ ☐
_____ ☐

notes:

_____
_____
_____
_____
_____

time	task	comments	status

things to do:

_____ ☐

_____ ☐

_____ ☐

_____ ☐

_____ ☐

_____ ☐

_____ ☐

_____ ☐

date
_____

_____ ☐

_____ ☐

_____ ☐

_____ ☐

_____ ☐

notes:

_____

_____

_____

_____

_____

time	task	comments	status

things to do:

_____ ☐
_____ ☐
_____ ☐
_____ ☐
_____ ☐
_____ ☐
_____ ☐
_____ ☐

date
_____

_____ ☐
_____ ☐
_____ ☐
_____ ☐
_____ ☐

notes:

_____
_____
_____
_____
_____

time	task	comments	status

things to do:

_____ ☐
_____ ☐
_____ ☐
_____ ☐
_____ ☐
_____ ☐
_____ ☐
_____ ☐

date
____

_____ ☐
_____ ☐
_____ ☐
_____ ☐
_____ ☐

notes:

_____
_____
_____
_____
_____

time	task	comments	status

things to do:

_____ ☐
_____ ☐
_____ ☐
_____ ☐
_____ ☐
_____ ☐
_____ ☐
_____ ☐

date
____

_____ ☐
_____ ☐
_____ ☐
_____ ☐
_____ ☐

notes:

_____
_____
_____
_____
_____

time	task	comments	status

things to do:

_____ ☐
_____ ☐
_____ ☐
_____ ☐
_____ ☐
_____ ☐
_____ ☐
_____ ☐

date
_____

_____ ☐
_____ ☐
_____ ☐
_____ ☐
_____ ☐

notes:

_____
_____
_____
_____
_____

time	task	comments	status

things to do:

_____ ☐
_____ ☐
_____ ☐
_____ ☐
_____ ☐
_____ ☐
_____ ☐
_____ ☐

date
_____

_____ ☐
_____ ☐
_____ ☐
_____ ☐
_____ ☐

notes:

_____
_____
_____
_____
_____

time	task	comments	status

things to do:
_____ ☐
_____ ☐
_____ ☐
_____ ☐
_____ ☐
_____ ☐
_____ ☐
_____ ☐

date
_____

_____ ☐
_____ ☐
_____ ☐
_____ ☐
_____ ☐

notes:
_____
_____
_____
_____
_____

time	task	comments	status

things to do:

_____ ☐
_____ ☐
_____ ☐
_____ ☐
_____ ☐
_____ ☐
_____ ☐
_____ ☐

date
_____

_____ ☐
_____ ☐
_____ ☐
_____ ☐
_____ ☐

notes:

_____
_____
_____
_____
_____

time	task	comments	status

things to do:

_____ ☐
_____ ☐
_____ ☐
_____ ☐
_____ ☐
_____ ☐
_____ ☐
_____ ☐

date
____

_____ ☐
_____ ☐
_____ ☐
_____ ☐
_____ ☐

notes:

_____
_____
_____
_____
_____

time	task	comments	status

www.ingramcontent.com/pod-product-compliance
Lightning Source LLC
Chambersburg PA
CBHW08073625626
47170CB00010B/2849